MW00618838

tanka 2020
poems from today's world

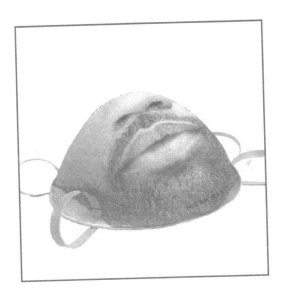

Alexis Rotella, Editor-in-Chief
Introduction by Michael McClintock

tanka 2020

foreword copyright © 2020 Alexis Rotella
introduction copyright © 2020 Michael McClintock
poems copyright © 2020 Red Moon Press
for the individual poets

ISBN 978-1-947271-60-9

Red Moon Press
PO Box 2461
Winchester VA
22604-1661 USA
www.redmoonpress.com

first printing

to those suffering,

and those fighting back

– *tanka 2020* editorial board –

Randy Brooks

Susan Burch

Tom Clausen

Margaret Chula

Marilyn Shoemaker Hazelton

Michael McClintock

Alexis Rotella

David Terelinck

Table of Contents

Foreword

At the Haiku North America 2019 conference in Winston-Salem, Jim Kacian asked if I'd curate Red Moon Press's second tanka anthology.[1] I agreed but decided it was a project that would require the input of other tanka poets. I put together a team of seven superlative poets and editors including Randy Brooks, Susan Burch, Tom Clausen, Maggie Chula, Marilyn Shoemaker Hazelton, Michael McClintock, and David Terelinck. Each poet brings to the table different life experiences and sensitivities.

tanka 2020 differs from the first Red Moon tanka anthology in that the focus of the poems relates to the challenging times that many of us didn't see coming. It's clear from reading the work that people the world over are concerned about climate change, the political scene and the disrespect of Nature as well as how we relate to one another.

In *the tanka anthology* (2003), a number of poets' sharings include a fair number of tanka representative of an individual's work, but in 2020, there are many more people writing. For that reason, we limited

---

1. *the tanka anthology*, edited by Michael McClintock, Pamela Miller Ness and Jim Kacian, Red Moon Press, appeared in 2003.

the number of poems in the main section of the anthology to no more than two per person. Each editor asked poets they admired to submit only seven poems, one or two which were chosen for the first cut by each respective editor. Afterwards all eight persons perused the entire list. We decided unanimously that only those tanka that received five votes and above would be included in the second and last cut.

Each editor's contribution was invaluable. Special appreciation to Marilyn Shoemaker Hazelton, editor of *Red Lights*, for her keen insights as well her final polishing of the manuscript; to Michael McClintock who took on the introduction; a deep bow to David Terelinck who drafted the submissions letter; and to Maggie Chula for offering to proofread the entire manuscript (along with Susan Burch), which was a laborious job. A deep bow also to Tom Clausen for collecting the credits and for other grunt work along the way. A thank you to long-time *Mayfly* editor Randy Brooks who came on board when needed late in the process. Lastly, this anthology would not exist without publisher Jim Kacian's vision.

— *Alexis Rotella*

Introduction

Truth has a thousand faces and contradictory versions of facts and information are amplified, spun and distorted by social media and instantaneous digital communications. What is projected as fact or truth disintegrates into free-for-all chaos, vulnerable to manipulation by the unseen, unknown, and any person.or group with an agenda and cause.

To address these conflicts and fractures, alarms and fears, we wanted as editors to gather a fair sample from a core of active, widely read tanka poets. The brevity and compactness of the tanka form eschew most of the noise encountered in poetry that relies on rhetoric, diatribe and rant. There are not enough lines in a tanka to work up that much locomotive steam (or gas).

tanka 2020 is the result. It is not a large collection but it is, we believe, representative, a kind of petition or evidential catalogue furnished by witnesses and set before us all. It may not be the book we set out to make but it is the book the poets wrote, gave us, and intended that we read. We are happy that our own poems are part of the conversation.

All the crimes and catastrophes that plague humanity riddle the period, some with new, startling variations. And when we look to other times and find a thinker like Albert Camus saying "I'm filled with a desire for clarity and meaning within a world and condition that offers neither" (in *The Myth of Sisyphus*), or an analytical idealist like G. W. F. Hegel concluding "What we learn from history is that we learn nothing from history", profound discouragement appears justified, maybe inescapable. In our time, George Floyd's "I can't breathe" polishes the mirror into which we all gaze, watching the cell phone video of his murder by police on a Minneapolis street.

Almost all poetry comes from troubled times. But poetry itself changes nothing. Statues will be toppled and new statues erected. Poets and readers alike are not passive observers. There are poems in this collection that may indeed transform awareness and consciousness, some human truth at the center of most of them. Poetry acts as a witness. That's what this book does.

— *Michael McClintock*

tanka 2020

man's footsteps
the imprints
that have
been left
in emptiness

Jenny Ward Angyal

orange tape
fluttering at the edge
of the clearcut
a doe and her fawn
pause between worlds

eastern puma
declared extinct —
a cry
from the dark mountain
tingles down my spine

an'ya

twilit rocks
the darkling beetles
in a crevice
night falls and morning rises
and everything starts over

how many times
I've crushed autumn leaves
until today
when a chickadee drank
from one that cupped the rain

Fay Aoyagi

sea anemone –
once I knew
how to weave
the moonlight
any way I wanted

the watch stopped
at 8:15 am
in Hiroshima . . .
thousands of origami cranes
waiting for the wind

Hifsa Ashraf

contemplating
near the border
a constellation
that connects the stars
at both sides

John Barlow

weary
of the same old thoughts . . .
the scrape
of eucalyptus leaves
on the peeling wall

days
since it fell to earth
I lift
the blackbird's lightness
into spring air

Roberta Beary

a child slaves
in basement squalor
weaving fragments of
the american dream
made in china

Jannick Belleau

swallows
in the waterfall
quench their thirst and bathe –
the orphan girl asks
is this like one big family?

day after day
picking up waste
on streets –
he cares for the planet
whether anyone sees him or not

Maxianne Berger

white cranes
spreading wings
warily
this precarious balance
between us

home
from the hospital
my neighbor
raking away dead leaves
in her stone garden

Michelle Brock

old-growth forest
the last mountain ash
cut down –
nothing now to brush
the clouds across the sky

he rubs his knee
along the young girl's thigh
under the table . . .
another violation
masquerades as a smile

Randy Brooks

just like that
two thumps
against the glass
one of us now
a widow

first the eyes
then the gestures
of her hands
how long can I pretend
not to understand?

Donna Buck

mother late for pickup –
in her daughter's lunch box
an "I love you" note
the girl tells me, *por si
la migra roundup*

Marjorie Buettner

he tells me
what to do if he dies
thinking ahead
my mind wanders inward
boat-drifting under the stars

Susan Burch

a Rubik's cube twisted
into a colorful mix –
what if we could
love ourselves
just the way we are?

on the plane
we're packed in
like sardines . . .
rubbing elbows
with everyone

Pris Campbell

fellowship tables
open for inbred believers
yet Sunday doors
so fast to slam shut
to the gender benders

James Chessing

had I learned to dance,
to tell a joke, to laugh,
or just to listen –
the sparrows come and go
as if I'm not here

he doesn't talk
about it,
the world inside –
a volcano
a peony

Sonam Chhoki

a blush of peonies
in the still-bare garden . . .
when I least expect it
this whimsical pulse
of new longings

toppled by the quake
the shrine we used to visit
now, the wind
in the broken bronze bell
rings in the new year

Margaret Chula

after hip surgery
the click, click, click of my cane
at Trader Joe's –
so many offers of help
from strangers older than me

refugees huddle
in makeshift shelters –
stench of mold
and urine-soaked mattresses
seep into their dreams

Marion Clarke

in Santiago
they convene again
for climate change
is anything really new
under this burning sun?

Tom Clausen

ambivalence
I believe is what
I've come to, sitting here
watching wave after wave
land itself

Kathy Lippard Cobb

on oxygen
mother lights
a cigarette –
part of me wants her
to explode

now and then
I still like a fairy tale
but the white knight is late
and these days
I'll put my faith in the horse

Susan Constable

another acre
of old-growth trees
felled and sold –
nature, our greatest neighbor
driven out of town

my train of thought
interrupted by the news –
two ideologies
coming down the track
in opposite directions

Magdalena Dale

green tea
in old porcelain cups –
a bygone era
when life was a poem
waiting to be written

Janet Lynn Davis

earthrise
from a lunar module
. . . how far
must we travel
to see what we have?

past midnight
the distant pop-pop-popping
of a firearm –
startling how unstartled
I've become about such things

Tish Davis

to the stranger's twenties
we strangers add ours
all the groceries
their mom had to pull back
moving again

my spoon
tapping a can
for the feral cats;
my brother, homeless,
in an unnamed woods

Cherie Hunter Day

just when I thought
I was unapproachable
you move closer
then everywhere
the sudden kindle of green

so few women
make careers in science
through a microscope
the beauty of an amoeba
as it changes shape

Margaret Dornaus

harvest moon
a barred owl's plaintive call
fills the night
as I dream of caged children
crying out for true love

another
mass shooting today
only crickets
speaking up for peace
in this war-torn world

Marje A Dyck

jaded, misguided
on a path
to destruction
we pick wildflowers
and gaze at the moon

Kirsten Cliff Elliot

not knowing
which way to turn, nor
how to forgive . . .
this sunlight always
finds a way through

sipping coffee
to the sound of dead leaves
sweeping across the path . . .
my definition of success
changing day by day

Jeanne Emrich

it is not age
we speak of
but the collapse
of bridges that
once carried us

Margarita Engle

assisted living –
my sister and I take the tour
for our parents
while wondering
about ourselves

Claire Everett

shaman
and medicine man
tanka by tanka
we work with ash
from the sacred fire

more headlines
for the climate change skeptics
Sunday morning
I listen harder for the words
to the robin's song

Ignatius Fay

changing face
of an older neighborhood
contrasts
ivy-covered stone
under solar roofs

sidewalk
outside the store
two teens
berate their parents
for littering

Amelia Fielden

dove trees blossom
in a nation that threatens war
yet again –
the complacent faces
on Independence Day

diner sign
limiting each stay
to half an hour
lest the poor linger
over a packet of fries

Jan Foster

westerly winds
carrying the choking dust
once again
some poor farmer's topsoil
lands in our backyard

huddled forms
along the shop fronts
this need
to sleep in daylight
shutting out the world

William Scott Galasso

acid rain
the tears that roll
from eyes to chin
when prayers
cannot stop bullets

why worry?
when I'm gone
the sun will rise, birds sing,
stars shine and our souls
will live together in peace

Barry George

I watch his latex fingers
wrap the sandwich
and count out my change
where once we trusted
one another's hands

I've wandered
in a snow globe forest
shaken
and turned upside down
. . . settling again

Beverley George

out there
in this war-torn world
people who
collect stamps, press flowers
gather shells at daybreak

LeRoy Gorman

ashes
in a Harley
urn
my uncle's
smooth ride on

white supremacists
in muscle shirts
the snow
can't come
soon enough

Grix

nothing left
of my childhood beaches . . .
grieving memories
that wash away
with the coastline

between pink & blue,
beautiful variations
of violet –
the gender identities
skirted by society

Autumn Noelle Hall

one by one
we pluck the sacred jewels
from Indra's Web
securing our own place
on the endangered species list

Hazel Hall

half asleep
I reach out and touch you
memories
of loved wash off
with soap and water

a label
on a small bottle –
drop by drop
discovering
what a placebo costs

Michele L Harvey

a sad betrayal
of all which we hold dear . . .
the mother's eyes
as she lets her child sip
a cup of tainted water

the lowering swoop
of the vulture's search
for the hit and run . . .
in this town where frackers
came and went overnight

Tia Haynes

reviewing
this week's paycheck
an error
in the value
of my gender

Marilyn Shoemaker Hazelton

already
the cherry trees
are counting
days & nights
before budding

if I could be
a flower next time
I would be clover –
that workhorse of beauty
blossoming everywhere

Gail Hennessy

what to pack
as the sun turns copper
first
the canary in its cage
so there will be singing

Christopher Herold

Quid Pro Quo
the name of that tall ship
now coming about
a silhouette under full sail
through the sun's glare

a flock of starlings
forms a Moebius strip . . .
we watch and listen
to the jazz of Chick Corea
and return to forever

Josie Hibbing

a little ball
of lemongrass floats
in the fish broth . . .
my childhood memories
of being poor

Ruth Holzer

if I didn't
beat my head against the wall
at least once a day
I wouldn't remember
who I am

Elinor Pihl Huggett

gale force wind
the constant clatter
of an open gate
scores of women
confront their abuser

in the big city
extended summer heat
the police captain
orders
more rape kits

Carol Judkins

what more
can we wish for –
this pink lotus
rising from a muddy pond
unfurling its fragrance

Jim Kacian

what I say next
will either be just right
or just wrong
let us trust the one
and accept the other

Kirsty Karkow

nowadays . . .
plastic bottles, paper cups
strewn thoughtlessly
beside our country road
why don't walkers notice?

the wheelchair
with a bent old woman . . .
an apparition
reflected in our window
that can't possibly be me!

Jet Keene

we owe a lot
to ships full
of crazy people
unafraid
of the edge

Julie Bloss Kelsey

handing over my drink
the barista recounts
coming out to his father
such unexpected intimacy
from a daily iced latte

at the book festival
the woman selling
religious inspiration
gives everyone
the evil eye

Mary Kendall

who am I
to judge you
without knowing
why you built
your fence?

Michael Ketchek

rusty railroad bridge
an antiwar slogan
painted forty years ago
still stands out
today

The caged tiger
pacing back and forth
I whisper
"listen big guy
it ain't great out here either"

Larry Kimmel

on my back
on a bed
in a bed and breakfast –
my dim destiny
mapped on a cracked ceiling

always fascinated by
that last half-inch in the long crawl
of evolution
where mankind straightens
to step out of the picture

Mariko Kitakubo

happiness –
they don't know
any other water,
tiny frogs are singing
at the source of River Hime

sounds
of the stream
in my homeland –
strontium is soaking
into the placenta

Kathy Kituai

some moments
are so easily mistaken
as ordinary
rescue cat licking
her open hand

my neighbor
revs his car at all hours
buys a Rottweiler
says he wants to shift
from this unsafe noisy street

Philomene Kocher

a week since the close call
I stop to watch birds bathing
in a puddle
& am stunned by the beauty
sun-lit drops of water

the fake pearl has worn off
the glass beads
of my First Communion rosary
I hold their innocence
in my hands

Shrikaanth Krishnamurthy

a bindi
and two long plaits
for the boy
the difference
between life and death

an ant on a twig
caught in the eddy –
an X
inscribed on the doors
of illegal aliens

Robert Kusch

losing the markers
of the red-oak trail
. . . the deep-rooted quiet
of everything
that outlives us

power outage:
in total darkness
we search for
each other's hand
– the warmth

Jessica Malone Latham

Earth
laughs in flowers
for hours
along the meadow
unable to catch my breath

mother's head
adorned with daisies
that time
when love was
all she needed

Michael H Lester

overnight
a violet vanishes
from its vase
in its place, a note
dripping with sarcasm

Angela Leuck

spring temperatures
skyrocket
around the world
59 Tomahawk missiles
streak to their target

convicted
of raping and killing
an 18-year-old girl,
the boy who lived
on Happy Valley Road

Antoinette Libro

sunrise services
a flock of white ibis
rising together
our morning prayer
over the marshes

Chen-ou Liu

my roommate reads
and rereads a letter
from Syria . . .
between us, dead silence
and a bottle of wine

under the banner
of the Green New Deal
a pink-haired girl
face to face
with a Trump cutout

Greg Longenecker

Ferris wheel
at the church carnival
I ride to
the farthest reaches
of childhood

chilly morning
he rises late
from his bed
on the church's
front steps

Bob Lucky

at their wedding
the couple vow to reduce
their carbon footprint
    after the honeymoon
        after the honeymoon

Jeanne Lupton

crossing the Bay Bridge
with a friend who fears heights
I do not mention
that once, in despair
I stopped my car just here and jumped

Carole MacRury

at its warmest
the worry stone I carry
day to day
fires, floods, chaos
and oceans rising

in between news
of violence, corruption
and climate change
Alexa and I make
chocolate chip cookies

Konno Mari

laid on my palm
a Jurassic fossil
so still –
to us is entrusted
the future

Joy McCall

what if
it all goes wrong?
says Piglet
what if it doesn't?
answers Pooh

Michael McClintock

One at a time,
I step on stones
and cross the stream –
when I'm across, the stones
go back to what they were doing

visiting hour . . .
an inmate's rough hands
cradle a photo
the guard pushes to him
on a stainless steel tray

Don Miller

a stone
next to a frozen pond
I long to skip
to another time
another place

all the children
holding pinwheels . . .
imagine
harnessing the power
in their hands

Robert Miller

the myth
of creation tales told
by campfire
legends lost in the glow
from smartphones

Vasile Moldovan

on the deck
of a ship with refugees
some teenagers
are waving the flag
of the promised country

ignoring again
the state of war
above the troops
a flock of pigeons
continues to fly

Mike Montreuil

a job always
hard to land –
his cap open
to a few dollars
and cigarettes

is that you
following a shadow
through the streets
of fitful sleep
I am here too

Joanne Morcom

after the bomb blast
the cellist seats himself
carefully in the ruins
he plays calming music
for all within earshot

Ron C Moss

the birdsong
I knew yesterday
will soon be gone
when one more species
has left this world

Pamela Miller Ness

A bud
of the red anemone
ready to burst . . .
the child
she never bore

Night
of thunder, thunder
in the dream
we fold laundry,
Mother and I.

Victor Ortiz

E pluribus unum . . .
one by one
stars
surface
from another world

Kathe L Palka

where once a roof arched
over this ruined stone church
a canopy
of leaves now shades me
as I revisit my faith

wind howls
the barometer drops
as tides rise
lives scatter
like leaves

Vandana Parashar

watering a bonsai
in juvenile home . . .
how does it feel
to blossom
uninhibited

scattered pieces
of limbs
as far as the eyes see . . .
when did we stop
being human

Marianne Paul

whispers
the boy next door
hanged himself
what darkness makes a flower
decide not to bloom

another forest
razed
for condos
the gridlock of streets
named after trees

Claudia Coutu Radmore

that our world
has the strength to hold on
like the red-leaf oxalis
which almost dead
revives in rain

Carol Raisfeld

blessings
from street sleepers
tucked in shadows
as I bring blankets
from the local church

sickened
seeing this child in a cage
so cold
a guard's voice says again
the wall will keep you warm

Kala Ramesh

tiger tiger
dwindling rapidly –
my grandchild
one day will know you
only from pictures

David Rice

huge decline
in bird populations
I need to do more
than keep our cats
indoors

Andrew Riutta

I've been to war,
and I have seen the Devil
in my enemy's eyes . . .
but never have I had to drink
the water in Flint.

Another mass shooting
over the car radio
as I work on the brakes
and dream of what's for lunch:
white bread and pickled hocks

Ce Rosenow

friend after friend
colleague after colleague
relative after relative
why didn't I post it?
#MeToo

print media
broadcast media
social media . . .
my prayer too
a kind of echo chamber

Alexis Rotella

Traces of Fukushima
in California wines -
a butterfly flaps its wings
in New Jersey
and a glacier starts to melt

Her husband in hospital –
still the farm woman
leaves a bowl of stew
and a slice of apple pie
on the new widow's stoop

Natalia L Rudychev

the wind is spinning
the prayer wheel
of moon
give me a hand
and I will move the earth

warm sunlight
on a temple door
too heavy
to pull open
with one hand

Miriam Sagan

election day –
still yellow leaves,
where will this sculpture
of a Native woman
be in a thousand years?

Dan Schwerin

the moon sets
the water is cool
I pray
forgive us our debts
of silence

I could be more
down to earth
no one is pious
burying a friend
silenced by opioids

Adelaide B Shaw

crossing borders
pulled from home and friends
too young to know
anything but mama's hand
until pulled from that, as well

Caroline Skanne

this
earth needs
mending . . .
the soft warbles
of ravens

fluent
in the language
of dawn
a blackbird's song
becomes my mantra

Ken Slaughter

immigrant
lives matter –
at eighty-nine
Mom raises
her first protest sign

global warming
is a hoax –
a sign found
floating in the streets
of New York City

Cindy Smith

What will bend
can't be broken
I am knots and braids
twisted into
something stronger

Paul Smith

turning my heart
a deeper shade of blue
dusk sings
the crow's
sad song

I find comfort
here too –
at dawn
the dark epiphany
of rooks

Christina Sng

learning to cherish
every moment
with the ones I love
how long do we have
left on this dying world

unable to sleep
I rescue leaf cuttings
and propagate them
the future feels
an iota brighter

Sheila Sondik

rhodies bloom
in utmost profusion
this spring
in its extravagance
dares us to despair

all my devices
plugged in for the night
I'm free to dream
of the years I had babies
and no screens to nurture

Carmen Sterba

an out-of-body
experience
swept me upwards
mallards navigating
their way home

growing up
without a father
we shared a lake
just a rowboat
ride away

John Stevenson

the unknown man
who stared down the tanks –
we love him
and also, the one
who pulled him aside

outside
the cinema
a line
of people waiting
to be shot

Maria Steyn

summer gusts . . .
amidst political strife
house sparrows
still feed their chicks
in nests of feathers and string

where water
and lush green
were plenty
now only a rattling wind
surrounds rusty tractors

Iliyana Stoyanova

last rays of sunlight
dance in the hospice corridor
the tapping of crutches
and his old watch –
a syncopated music

lost
between two languages
fighting
my own demons
and yet . . . stardust

Celia Stuart-Powles

what we noticed
on the drive was
an absence of stars
from Dallas to Tulsa
. . . erased by lights

listening
as her memory
slips
the family ghosts
out of the closet

Alan Summers

lifting me away
from the computer
to my kitchen window
the early morning honks
of Canada geese

Carmel Summers

last year's stubble
where this year's crop should be
the sky stark blue
no swathes of green
to hide the black dog

Lesley Anne Swanson

climate strike
at the bottom of the 9th
no one
knows
how it will end

library fines
for a history book
the biography
of a tyrant
written in today's headlines

David Terelinck

bush retreat,
our cellphones collected
upon arrival
we connect and recharge
beneath a billion stars

2,000 likes
on facebook & twitter
virtually
all of my friends
are virtual

Michael Thorley

coal trucks
click past the crossing
a mantra
eighty-five times repeated
and I am enlightened

Julie Thorndyke

bone-dry days
warm westerly winds
we fade and fall
purple petals
crunched underfoot

how am I now
to navigate life?
one of the stars
by which I steer
has fallen

Kozue Uzawa

absorbing
black *sumi* ink
and her energy
the calligraphy paper
becomes a work of art

Margaret Van Every

passing tables
at a sidewalk café she asks
do any of you women
by any chance
need a cleaning lady?

Christine "Chrissi" L Villa

a solitary star
after a huge earthquake . . .
a child sleeps
at an evacuation center
with somebody's doll

Tamara K Walker

the way they pretended
their mechanical pencils were
hypodermic needles –
the foreshadowing
of youthful boredom

Karma Tenzing Wangchuk

A tall, sturdy tree
to lean my back against –
sometimes that's all
that I want in this world,
but the world comes with it

Linda Jeannette Ward

be a nameless stream
in an unnamed forest
murmuring mantras
accentuated only
by falling needles of pine

we're afloat
on this barrier island
glacier-calved waters
crash along every side
a broken bridge to nowhere

Michael Dylan Welch

shiny pens and a stapler –
no one tells
the new hire
his desk is where
the suicide sat

Don Wentworth

scattering
leaves at my feet
the breeze
raises the question
and answer at once

Neal Whitman

reading Homer
by the light of a waning moon
a glimpse of hope
one generation flowers
even as another withers

Steve Wilkinson

every faded leaf
of autumn –
the children
of war-torn countries
that no one cares for

Kath Abela Wilson

wearing green
a thousand welcoming
lady liberties with torches
at the airport
carrying poems

at 94 mom died hopeful
that the America she loved
had overcome racism . . .
she did not live
to see it didn't

Beatrice Yell

a massive task
to declutter papers
while the postman
stuffs my letterbox
with junk mail

Aya Yuhki

in the dense-leaved darkness
of this mountain isle,
there must be
unending struggles
for existence

J Zimmerman

Crammed bookshelves
yet I still seek
the perfect text
that teaches me
to dream in Japanese

On this pilgrimage
everything is missing
everyone is missing
still day after day I walk
higher into the hills

The Covid/Protest Supplement

Just as this anthology was about to go to press, Covid-19 burst forward with full fury. Three months later the brutality of a policeman knee-pressing the life out of George Floyd for nearly nine minutes was captured on camera. His death sparked a new awareness among the races. With the pandemic raging, people took to the streets in masks to support the Black Lives Matter movement (without the usual "All Lives" qualifier).

Despite the suffering and many deaths, the coronavirus cloud seemed to have a silver lining for a while. While people sheltered in place, smog cleared in many areas. Nature rallied absent the usual pollution. But as soon as the warmer weather set in, too many individuals relaxed. Beaches and bars opened and the number of cases spiked. Contrary to what some politicians promised, the virus was not diminished by warmer weather. The president of the United States refuses to wear a mask and tells his base the virus will fade like morning mist.

Some airlines are starting to sardine-pack passengers in again. Businesses reopened only to close right up again. Many people work from home in near isolation. Friends don't get together for dinner anymore. Except for a few governors and mayors, the old guard continues its denial despite scientific data.

Social media rants and outrage are at an all-time high. Use of the "f" word is getting old. To quote Rumi, "It's better to raise your words than raise your voice."

These are surreal times, to be sure. For way too many, the clock has unhappily run out. Suffering is immense. Who knows where we'll be when this anthology finally makes its debut? Who knows how the stars will align? Perhaps aliens will land. Maybe more people will pick up their pens and start to write poetry. We cannot allow masks to muffle our creativity.

— *Alexis Rotella*
Arnold Maryland

John Stevenson

not feeling good
or bad enough
for poetry
these days we all wonder
have I got the virus

Randy Brooks

baby toes
all five little pigs
stay home
to shelter
in place

Debbie Strange

rain doves build
a nest on our balcony
we, too
are learning the art
of sheltering in place

Randy Brooks

spring plague
holding hands
with nobody
under the blooming
cherry tree

Roberta Beary

arthritic hands
wipe down a doorbell
no one rings
this caterpillar
also cocooning

Jim Kacian

after years
of online dating
we finally meet
and she looks good
at a mere six feet

Jim Kacian

the difference
between self-isolation
and my usual life
is so subtle
I barely notice

Roberta Beary

across continents
my sister pretty in pink
our long feud forgotten
as we hand-stitch masks
from old lady panties

Kirsty Karkow

housebound –
rain and snowy days
don't help
no wonder fairy tales
told of magic wands

Kirsty Karkow

so kind
to see people place
bags of food
on her doorstep
refusing payment

David Terelinck

isolation
gifts us cleaner air
and waterways –
so much we can learn
from one small virus

Claire Everett

a silver key
to this lockdown dawn . . .
blackbird
the comfort you bring
to this troubled world

Maxianne Berger

wistful look
at the day's sunny dawn
sheltering at home
I awaken from a dream
about baseball

Carole MacRury

several months
of social distancing . . .
even my face
in the morning mirror
that of a stranger

Maggie Chula

hospital triage
for Covid19 victims
who should live or die –
in the dark forest
a swath of white trilliums

Kathe L Palka

cherry petals drift
in a grocery store lot
where garbage overflows
with discarded
gloves and masks

Susan Burch

Covid19 . . .
the shouting
between customers
over who gets
the last roll of TP

an'ya

over this long
period of quarantine
my plan to sell
material possessions
to buyers with more time left

an'ya

sparkling beach sand
how can I stand the sheer
beauty of it
when the glare of fake news
brings me daily to tears

Margaret Dornaus

self-isolating
how to explain the hunger
for what was once
the simplest of gestures
one hand touching another

James Chessing

we are swimmers
in an ocean of microbes
when you're blind
how to tell the shark
from the seal?

Cherie Hunter Day

in this war
the soldiers wear scrubs
and plead for masks
meanwhile respirators
go to the highest bidder

Alexis Rotella

Our president
in a frosty pink tie
tells reporters
you're all
a disgrace

Alexis Rotella

Protestors in front of
the White House
Trump hides
in a bunker
his pants on fire

Carol Raisfeld

a grim global virus
writing our destiny on the wind
alone with fear
telling fear to leave me alone
not knowing how it will end

James Chessing

it comes from wearing
a mask all day –
that sick feeling
re-breathing my own words
waiting for . . . what?

Maggie Chula

sheltering in place
my husband kneels
in the back yard
eradicating
the viral fireweed

Debbie Strange

empty cathedral . . .
he sings for everyone
and for no one
this moment of healing
in a quarantined world

(for Andrea Bocelli)

Debbie Strange

this curse
should be named
corvid19
the way it pecks
holes in our lungs

Terri Hale French

watching the news
dad says
the weather girl
is very pretty
for a black girl

2020

Robert Rotella

Pepper spray
rubber bullets
tear gas, batons –
thousands arrested
without water or masks

Robert Rotella

Memorial Day
another police officer
kneels on the neck
of a black man –
Lady Liberty weeps

Orrin Prejean

this day I will not
give away smiles
soft words or kind gestures
give me common human decency
or this Republic will burn

Orrin Prejean

fear of riots
fear of businesses burning
still no room in that heart
for fear of another
black body dying

Basha Ma

Another day of isolation –
a bag of peas bursts open
onto the floor . . .
why am I not out
protesting on the streets?

Basha Ma

Black Lives Matter
people of all colors
risk their lives
for justice –
only took 401 years

Debbie Strange

taking a knee . . .
the black hollyhocks
in my garden
fall victim, one by one
to another killing frost

Lori Minor

coronapocalypse
all the movies
I've seen
never prepared me
for this

Credits

"a bindi" — *red lights*, "1984" sequence (2019)

"A bud" — *Lilliput Review* 150 (July 2006)

"a job always" — *The Tanka Journal* 48 (2016)

"a label" — *Eucalypt* 26 (2019)

"a massive task" — *Ribbons* 13:3 (2017)

"a Rubik's cube twisted" — World Tanka Contest, Honorable Mention (July 2019)

"a stone" — *tinywords* 9:1 (2010)

"a week since the close call" — *Gusts* 16 (Fall/Winter 2012)

"absorbing" — *Ribbons* 13:3 (2017)

"after hip surgery" — *Ribbons* 15:2 "Tanka Café"

"all my devices" — Sanford Goldstein International Tanka Contest, Honorable Mention (2017)

"all the children" — *ATPO*, Special Feature: "Turn the Other Cheek"

"already" — *International Tanka* 5 (2019)

"always fascinated by" — *Simply Haiku* (May 15, 2008)

"ambivalence" — *Tangled Hair* 2 (2000)

"an ant on a twig" — *Haibun Today* (2017)

"an empty lot" — *Ash Moon Anthology* (2008)

"an out-of-body" — *Skylark* 5:2 (2017)

"another acre" — *Skylark* 7:1 (2019)

"ashes" — *Gusts* 26 (2017)

"at the book festival" — *Bamboo Hut* (Autumn 2016)

"at the bottom" — *ATPO* 34

"be a nameless stream" — *Blithe Spirit* 29.3 (2019)

"contemplating" — *cattails* (April 2019)

"Crammed bookshelves" — *Presence* (2019)

"crossing the Bay Bridge" — *Tanka Splendor* (?)

"day after day" — Original version in *Pour l'Amour de l'Autre* (2019)

"days" — British Haiku Society Awards, Winner (2015)

"diner sign" — *Baubles, Bangles, & Beads* (2007)

"Earth" — *Skylark* 5:2 (2017); italicized quote from Ralph Waldo Emerson

"eastern puma" — *cattails* (April 2018)

"fear of riots" — *Poets Salon*, June 2020
"first the eyes" — *Modern English Tanka* 3.2 (2008)

"gale force wind" — *Ribbons* 14:3 (2018)
"grandfather sleeps" — *Gusts* 29 (2018)
"green tea" — *Shore Lights* (2017)
"growing up" — *Ribbons* 13:2 (2017)

"had I learned to dance" — *Mariposa* 39 (2018)
"he doesn't talk" — *Skylark* 6:2 (2018)
"he tells me" — *Gusts* 14 (2011)

"I pretend" — *Eucalypt* 16 (2014)
"I watch his latex fingers" — *American Tanka* 28 (2017)
"if I could be" — *Gusts* 27 (2018)
"in full flight" — *Eucalypt* 16 (2014)
"in the big city" — *Ribbons* 14:2 (2018)
"is that you" — *Gusts* 20 (2014)
"I've never been homeless" — *bottle rockets* 12
"I've wandered" — *Gusts* 22 (2015)

"just when I thought" — *Kindle of Green* (2008)

"library fines" — *NeverEndingStory* (April 21, 2018)

"lifting me away" — *Blithe Spirit* 20:3 (2010)

"listening" — Tanka Society of America Poetry Contest, Honorable Mention (2014)

"losing the markers" — *Ribbons* 9:1 (2013)

"lost" — *Skylark* 3:2 (2015)

"mother late for pickup" — Colorado Boulevard Poetry Corner (March 2017)

"mother's head" — *bottle rockets* 35 (2016)

"my fingertips" — *Ash Moon Anthology* (2008)

"my neighbor" — *Straggling Into Winter* (2007)

"my spoon" — World Tanka Competition, First Place (2013)

"my train of thought" — *Hedgerow* 71 (2016)

"Nazis shot father" — *Ribbons* 11:2 (2015)

"Night" — *A Thousand Paper Cranes* (2006)

"not knowing" — *A Hundred Gourds* 3:3 (2014)

"now and then" — *Eucalypt* 17 (2014)

"old-growth forest" — *Ribbons* 11: 2 (2015)

"on my back" — *Modern English Tanka* 12 (2009)

"on oxygen" — *Presence* 44 (2011)

"on the plane" — *Gusts* 29 (2019)

"On this pilgrimage" — *red lights* 11:1 (2015)

"One at a time" — *red lights* 15:2 (2019)

"out there" — *Simply Haiku* 6:3 (2008)

"outside" — *Ribbons* 8.3 (2013)

"passing tables" — *Neon Graffiti* (July 2016)

"power outage" — *Ribbons* 15:4 (2019)

"rain puddle" — *Eucalypt* 25 (2018)

"raindrops" — *Gusts* 21 (2015)

"rusty railroad bridge" — *red lights* 14:2 (2018)

"shaman" — Honoring Oceti Sakowin, "Stand with Standing Rock" (February 23, 2017)

"sipping coffee" — *A Hundred Gourds* 3:1 (2013)

"some moments" — *Presence* 57, Best of Issue Award (2017)

"sounds" — *Rattle* 47

"swallows" — Original version in *Pour l'Amour de l'Autre* (2019)

"The caged tiger" — *red lights* 4:2 (2008)
"this day I will not" — *Poets Salon*, June 2020

Author Biographies

ai li is a Straits Chinese cherita, tanka and haiku poet from London and Singapore who writes about Life, Love and Loss bringing healing and prayer to her poems. She is the creator of cherita, editor and publisher of *the cherita*, founding editor and publisher of *still, moving into breath* and *dew-on-line*.

Jenny Ward Angyal lives with her husband and one Abyssinian cat on a small organic farm in Gibsonville, North Carolina. Having published in many journals, her tanka collection, *moonlight on water*, appeared in 2016.

an'ya is founding editor of of the Tanka Society of America journal *Ribbons*, founder of United Haiku and Tanka Society/first editor of *cattails*, founder/sole editor of *moonset literary newspaper*, and *haigaonline* editor. She has won many awards, including six times the British Haiku/Tanka Society Competitions.

Fay Aoyagi, originally from Tokyo, lives in San Francisco. She believes English-language tanka will become more diversified reflecting the different life-styles and culture treasured by her adopted country.

Award-winning poet, story writer, and co-editor of the Haiku Commentary blog, **Hifsa Ashraf** is from Rawalpindi, Pakistan. Her poems have been published worldwide. *https://hifsays.blogspot.com.* (*https://haikucommentary.wordpress.com/*)

John Barlow edited *Tangled Hair*, the first journal dedicated to English-language tanka to be published outside the United States. His tanka collection, *Snow About To Fall* (2006), was published by Snapshot Press.

Basha Ma is a citizen of the world.

Roberta Beary writes to connect with the disenfranchised, to let them know they are not alone. As Roving Ambassador for The Haiku Foundation, she facilitates community workshops worldwide and in County Mayo, Ireland, where she is the longtime haibun editor for *Modern Haiku.*

Janick Belleau, born and raised in Montréal, lived in Ottawa and Winnipeg before returning to her beloved city... with the love of her life. Her tanka and haiku collections, as well as presentations and literary reviews, can be viewed at site: *ps://janickbelleau.ca/.*

Montrealer **Maxianne Berger** contributes reviews and articles, in French and English, to tanka and haiku publications. With Mike Montreuil she co-edited two francophone tanka anthologies and, for six years, the on-line francophone journal *Cirrus: tankas de nos jours*. Her 2014 tanka collection *un renard roux/a red fox* (petits nuages) is bilingual.

Michelle Brock is a Canberra poet, short story writer and member of the Limestone Tanka Poets. She finds inspiration along rivers and beaches and in everyday moments.

Randy Brooks is Dean of Arts & Sciences at Millikin University. He and his wife **Shirley Brooks** are publishers of Brooks Books and co-editors of *Mayfly* haiku magazine. His most recent books include *Walking the Fence: Selected Tanka* and *The Art of Reading and Writing Haiku: A Reader Response Approach*, both published in 2019.

Donna Buck lives in Carlsbad, California. She is retired as director of a program for DACA students (Dreamers) whom she misses and continues to support. She is a social justice advocate and nature lover, both of which influence her poetry.

Marjorie Buettner has two books of poetry published by Red Dragonfly Press: *Seeing it Now* (Haiku and Tanka) and *Some Measure Of Existence* (haibun) which won the Haiku Society of America Book Award.

Susan Burch is a tanka and haiku writer from Hagerstown, Maryland and current Vice President of the Tanka Society of America. Her first book, *Angry Tanka*, was published in 2019 (*Lulu.com*).

Pris Campbell is a former clinical psychologist who also sailed and biked until a neuroimmune illness (ME/CFS) cut that life short in 1990. In this life, she writes and publishes short form and free verse poetry from the home she shares with her husband in Lake Worth, Florida.

The world inside is a large focus of tanka by **James Chessing**, a clinical psychologist. Having written haiku since 1970, he took up tanka in 2005 and won the Tanka Society of America Contest in 2010.

Principal editor, and co-editor of haibun for the United Haiku and Tanka Society journal *cattails*, **Sonam Chhoki** finds the Japanese short form poetry resonates with her Tibetan Buddhist upbringing.

She is inspired by her father, Sonam Gyamtsho, the architect of Bhutan's non-monastic modern education and by her mother, Chhoden Jangmu, who taught her: "Being a girl doesn't mean you can't do anything."

Margaret Chula served for five years as president of the Tanka Society of America. Her tanka collections include: *Always Filling, Always Full* (White Pine Press, 2001), *Just This* (Mountains & Rivers Press, 2013), and *Perigee Moon* (Red Mountain Press, 2020).

Writer and artist **Marion Clarke** is from the town of Warrenpoint, located on the east coast of Northern Ireland. One of her tanka received an honorable mention in the 2019 Sanford Goldstein International Tanka Contest; a second was published in December 2019 in *Atlas Poetica 39: A Journal of World Tanka*.

Tom Clausen lives in Ithaca, New York, where he enjoys daily walks to take photos and write little poems. He is a member of the Rt. 9 Haiku Group and curates a daily haiku feature at Albert R. Mann Library, Cornell University where he worked for over 35 years.

Kathy Lippard Cobb lives (with her furry peeps) in Bradenton, Florida and is an award-winning tanka poet published in journals all over the world. When

Kathy is not writing, it is not unusual to find her rescuing turtles from the roadside.

A current editor of the Canadian journal *Gusts*, **Susan Constable** has co-edited several haiku and tanka anthologies, and judged several haiku and tanka contests. She lives on British Columbia's beautiful west coast, where nature inspires her poetry.

Living in Bucharest, Romania, **Magdalena Dale** was a co-editor for the *Take Five* tanka anthologies. She has written two tanka books, a renga book together with the poet Vasile Moldovan and a book of string tanka with photos by Luminia Suse. She edited the first Romanian tanka anthology, *Rain of Stars*.

Janet Lynn Davis lives in a rustic area of southeast Texas, away from the hustle-bustle of the big city. Her tanka and related forms have appeared in numerous journals and anthologies; she also served in the tanka community in various capacities.

A resident of Northern Ohio, **Tish Davis**'s tanka and related forms have appeared in numerous online and hardcopy publications. When she isn't busy with work and grandchildren, she enjoys exploring the local parks with her husband and three dogs.

Associate Editor of *The Heron's Nest*, **Cherie Hunter Day** is a widely-published poet, a few works of which include the award-winning e-chapbook *A Color for Leaving* (Snapshot Press, 2017), and *Kindle of Green* (Platyopus Books/Swamp Press, 2008), a collection of responsive tanka with David Rice.

Margaret Dornaus was awarded first place in the Tanka Society of America's International Tanka Contest in 2011 for her poem "years from now". A widely-published writer, her book of haibun and tanka prose, *Prayer for the Dead*, received a Haiku Society of America Merit Book Award in 2017.

Living in Saskatchewan, Canada, **Marje A. Dyck**'s poetry collections include *rectangle of light* (proof press, 1996), *A Piece of the Moon* (Calisto Press, 2005) and *Still Blue Water* (Calisto Press, 2012). Her poetry, prose and sumi-e have appeared in numerous publications including *Loch Raven Review, Ribbons, Frogpond, Haiku Canada Review,* and *World Haiku Review.*

Kirsten Cliff Elliot has been writing and publishing Japanese short-form poetry since 2007. Her haiku were featured in *A New Resonance 8: Emerging Voices in English-Language Haiku* (Red Moon Press, 2013), and her first book, *Patient Property: a journey through leukemia* (Velvet Dusk Publishing, 2019), is a collection of both haiku and tanka.

Jeanne Emrich is a poet and artist living in Edina, Minnesota. She is founder of *tankaonline.com* (est. 2007) and author of *The Pleiades at Dawn: A Tanka Anthology* (2007).

Margarita Engle is a Cuban-American author who lives in Central California. Her most recent verse memoir is *Soaring Earth*. Her newest books include *Dancing Hands, Dreams From Many Rivers*, and *With a Star in My Hand*.

Claire Everett is the founder and editor of *Skylark* tanka journal and, for five years, was tanka prose editor at *Haibun Today*. When she's not writing poetry, she works with adults with autism, learning disabilities and complex needs, practicing yoga, or cycling the hills and dales of North Yorkshire, England.

Ignatius Fay, a disabled invertebrate paleontologist, writes haiku, tanka, haibun and tanka prose. The current editor of the Haiku Society of America *Bulletin* and layout artist for *Frogpond*, Ignatius resides in Sudbury, Ontario, Canada.

Amelia Fielden is an Australian, a professional translator of traditional Japanese poetry forms in English, who has produced 22 books of translation. She is also a writer of traditional Japanese poetry forms, with eight of her own such collections in print, the most recent being *These Purple Years* (2018).

Writer and editor **Terri L French** is past Southeast Regional Coordinator for The Haiku Society of America. She served as editor of *Prune Juice Journal* of *senryu* and *kyoka* and was on the editorial team of *Haibun Today*. Currently Terri is on the editorial team of *contemporary haibun online* and a member-at-large of the board of The Haiku Foundation.

Jan Foster, a retired English teacher, lives in Geelong, in country Victoria, Australia. She is a distance member of the Bottlebrush Tanka Group.

William Scott Galasso is author of sixteen books of poetry including *Mixed Bag (A Travelogue in Four Forms)* (2018), and *Rough Cut: Thirty Years of Senryu* (2019) available on Amazon. He edited *Eclipse Moon* (2017), the 20th Anniversary issue of Southern California Haiku Study Group.

Barry George, an AWP Intro Poets Award recipient and Pushcart nominee, has won numerous short-form competitions, including First Prize in the Gerald R. Brady Senryu Contest. Published in numerous venues, he lives and teaches in Philadelphia.

Beverley George was founder/editor of *Eucalypt: a Tanka Journal* (2006–2016) and is current editor of *Windfall: Australian Haiku*. She was President of the Australian Haiku Society from 2006–10 and convenor of the 4th Haiku Pacific Conference 2009.

LeRoy Gorman's poetry, much of it visual and minimalist, has appeared in various publications and exhibitions worldwide and has garnered numerous awards including, most recently, the 2017 Dwarf Stars Award. His newest book, *goodwill galaxy hunting* was published by Urban Farmhouse Press in 2019.

Grix (they/them) is an award-winning Pushcart-nominated writer and visual artist whose work focuses on disability, gender, trauma, and systems from a neurodiverse perspective. They are the Founder and Editor-in-Chief for *Human/Kind Journal*.

Autumn Noelle Hall writes from a cedar cabin in Green Mountain Falls, Colorado, a skipping-stone'sthrow from a waterfall where thirsty deer, bobcats, mountain lions and bears come to drink. It's their world as much as her own that she longs to preserve.

Hazel Hall is a versatile Australian poet. Her latest books are *Step By Step* (Picaro Press, 2018), *Severed Web* (Picaro Press, 2020) and *Moonlight Over the Siding* (Interactive Press, 2019).

Michele L Harvey is a professional landscape painter in New York, dividing her time between both city and country. She has been writing tanka and haiku since 2005 and examples of her work can be found on her website: *micheleharvey.com*.

Tia Haynes was featured in *New Resonance 11: Emerging Voices in English-Language Haiku* and lives in Lakewood, Ohio, with her husband and two daughters. When not writing poetry she enjoys vegan cuisine and theater of all kinds.

Marilyn Shoemaker Hazelton, based in Allentown, Pennsylvania, edits *red lights*, an international tanka journal. A past president of the Tanka Society of America, her writing has been published internationally. She is a teaching artist who reads and writes tanka for inspiration and insight.

Gail Hennessy is an Australian poet whose tanka have appeared in *Eucalypt: A Tanka Journal, Grevillia & Wonga Vine Australian Tanka of Place* and the online journal *Echidna Tracks*.

Christopher Herold has been writing in the *haikai* genres for more than fifty years. He is a past president of the Haiku Poets of Northern California and co-founder of *The Heron's Nest* haiku journal for which he served as managing editor from 1999–2007.

Josie Hibbing is a native from the Philippines. She lives in Iowa with her husband and eight children.

Ruth Holzer's haiku, tanka and haibun have appeared in many journals and anthologies. She has published five chapbooks of longer poetry and received nominations for the Pushcart Prize.

Elinor Pihl Huggett began writing haiku in 2005 and, in 2008 started teaching haiku and related forms to seniors in South Bend, Indiana. In 2018 she won the Touchstone Award for Individual Poems.

Carol Judkins lives near the ocean in California. Her work has appeared in numerous journals and anthologies, and in her chapbook, *at the water's edge*.

Jim Kacian is founder and director of The Haiku Foundation, founder and owner of Red Moon Press, editor-in-chief of *Haiku in English: The First Hundred Years* (W.W. Norton, 2013), and co-editor of *the tanka anthology* (Red Moon Press, 2003).

Kirsty Karkow discovered haiku and tanka, along with other Asian poetry in 2000, which have brought her much joy ever since. She lives on the coast of Maine with many lovely views for inspiration.

Jet Keene teaches American literature and studies in California preparatory high schools. He founded the San Joaquin Valley Poets in 2014, dedicated to study and writing modern short poetry forms, including contemporary English-language haiku and tanka.

Julie Bloss Kelsey writes short-form poetry from her home in suburban Maryland. Twitter (*@MamaJoules*) and Instagram (*@julieblosskelsey*).

Mary Kendall, a resident of Chapel Hill, North Carolina, is author of two books. Her poetry has been published in many print and online poetry journals. Mary's poetry blog is called "A Poet in Time" at: *http://www.apoetintime.com*.

Frogpond Editor **Michael Ketchek** went door to door in 1972 collecting signatures for Shirley Chisholm's presidential campaign.

Writing for over 40 years, **Larry Kimmel** was born in Johnstown, Pennsylvania. He lives quietly in the hills of western Massachusetts. He holds degrees from Oberlin Conservatory and Pittsburgh University, and has worked at everything from steel mills to libraries.

Mariko Kitakubo from Japan is a tanka poet/performer who has published six books, including three bilingually. She has presented her poetry on at least 238 occasions, 177 of them overseas in 51 cities.

Kathy Kituai is the founder of Limestone Tanka Poets, and tanka editor for *Cattails* (2018 – 19). Her fourth tanka book, *Deep in the Valley of Teabowls* won the 2016 ACT Publishing & Writing Award.

Fascinated by voice and possibility, **Philomene Kocher** began writing haiku in 1991 and tanka in 2001. Her poetry has been published internationally.

Shrikaanth Krishnamurthy's haikai and tanka poems have been published in many journals of repute. He edits and publishes *ephemerae*.

Robert Kusch taught American literature for 39 years at Rutgers University. He has a long-standing interest in Japanese poetry, and has written tanka since 1996.

Jessica Malone Latham is an award-winning poet, and mother of two boys. She most recently worked with Brooks Books as editor of *Another Trip Around the Sun: 365 Days of Haiku for Children Young and Old*.

Michael H Lester is a CPA and attorney living in Los Angeles, California. Michael's work has been widely published in many poetry journals and has won numerous awards worldwide.

Angela Leuck is the author of *More Grows in A Crooked Row* — a collection of tanka conversations with 15 Canadian poets. She lives in Hatley, Quebec.

Antoinette Libro, retired Professor Emerita from Rowan University, divides her time between St. Augustine, Florida and Sea Isle City, New Jersey. Her chapbooks include *The Carpenter's Lament in Winter*.

Chen-ou Liu lives in Ajax, Ontario, Canada. He is the author of two award-winning books, and his tanka and haiku have been honored with many awards.

An award-winning poet in Pasadena, California, **Gregory Longenecker**, writes primarily Japanese short forms, including tanka. He's a member of many haikai groups and has judged several contests.

Bob Lucky is author of *My Theology: Not Always True But Always Truth* (Cyberwit, 2019) and two chapbooks of haibun and prose poems. He splits his time between Saudi Arabia, where he works, and Portugal, where he doesn't.

Poet and writer **Jeanne Lupton**'s tanka have been published internationally over the past 25 years. She lives in senior housing in Berkeley, California, where she leads a weekly memoir writing group.

Carole MacRury resides in Point Roberts, Washington, a unique peninsula and border town that inspires her work. She is the author of *In the Company of Crows: Haiku and Tanka Between the Tides* (Black Cat Press, 2008, 2nd Printing, 2018) and *The Tang of Nasturtiums*, an award-winning e-chapbook (Snapshot Press, 2012).

Konno Mari lives in Fukui City, Japan. She is a member of the editorial committee of *Mirai* journal, and editor-in-chief of *International Tanka*. Her book *Snow Crystal * Star-shaped* (*Hoshijo-rokka*), contains tanka in Japanese, with English and Latvian translations (English translations by Amelia Fielden).

Joy McCall, a prolific poet, refers to poetry as her saving grace. A paraplegic amputee following a motorcycle crash which ended her nursing work, Joy lives in Norwich, England.

Michael McClintock's career in tanka and haiku began in the 1960s in Los Angeles, where he was born, and continues today in the San Joaquin Valley and on the slopes of the Sierra. He is author of the "Tanka Cafe" for *Ribbons*, journal of the Tanka Society of America.

Don Miller lives in the Chihuahuan Desert of southern New Mexico. He has been writing tanka since the early 1980s. His tanka, tanka sequences, tanka prose, and other short-form poetry have been published in various journals since the early 2000s.

Robert Miller elected not to supply a biography.

Living in Bucharest, Romania, **Vasile Moldovan** has published tanka poems in many international journals including *Aha!*, *Atlas Poetica*, *Moonset*, *Ribbons*, and *Simply Haiku*. He has published two tanka books:

After the tempest (2013) and *Between sky and earth* (2019) as well as five haiku booklets, a historical novel and a book of renku (with Magdalena Dale).

Mike Montreuil's haiku, tanka, and haibun, written in English and in French, have been published in various print and on-line journals. Mike is the editor of the *Haiku Canada Review* and was co-editor (with Maxianne Berger) of the online journal *Cirrus: Tanka de nos jours*, from 2012 – 2019.

Joanne Morcom is a short-form poet and social worker in Calgary, Alberta, Canada. Author of four poetry collections, she collaborates with the Nikka Yuko Japanese Garden in Lethbridge, Alberta to lead haiku workshops.

Ron C Moss is a Tasmanian poet and artist whose haiku and short-form poetry have appeared in leading journals and anthologies round the world. His award-winning poems and haiku collections have been featured many times and translated into several languages. Ron's latest collection, *Broken Starfish*, is available from him at *ronmoss8@gmail.com*.

Resident of Rochester, New York, **Pamela Miller Ness**'s life's journey centers around teaching, writing, and making art. She divides her time between volunteering at Rochester's Memorial Art Gallery and creating fiber art, which she donates to a variety of non-profits supporting Special Olympics athletes, veterans, cancer care, and local arts organizations.

Living in Bellingham, Washington, **Victor Ortiz** earned his Ph.D. in Classics from UCLA. He shares his poetry with a wide range of audiences, and enjoys collaborating with poets, artists, and scholars.

In 2015 Red Moon Press published *A Path of Desire*, tan renga written by **Kathe L Palka** and Peter Newton. In 2011 she won an eChapbook Award from Snapshot Press for her tanka collection *As the Years Pass*. She has been an editor for *tinywords* since 2011.

Vandana Parashar is a published poet of haiku, senryu, tanka, haiga and haibun. She has won prizes and honorable mentions in many contests.

Marianne Paul is a Canadian poet and novelist. When she's not playing with words, she dabbles in bookbinding, visual art, and gentle kayaking. She is the author of *Body Weight*, a collection of poetry and art published by Human/Kind Press.

Orrin Prejean lives in Dallas, Texas USA. He's a tale-weaver who enjoys the shortness of ku and ka with which to tell stories.

Claudia Coutu Radmore is the author of *Your Hands Discover Me/ Tes mains me découvrent*, and *fish spine picked clean*. She is president of Haiku Canada.

Carol Raisfeld, a worldwide anthologized poet and winner of many international awards, lives in Atlantic Beach, New York. Her poetry, art and photography appear in numerous print and online journals.

Kala Ramesh was on the editorial board of *Take Five: The Best Contemporary Tanka* 2009, 2010 and 2011. Her book of tanka, tanka prose and tanka dohe will be published by Harper Collins in July 2020.

David Rice was editor of *Ribbons*, the journal of the Tanka Society of America, from 2012 – 2019. He lives in Berkeley, California, with his wife, three children, and three grandchildren who live nearby.

Published in many venues, **Andrew Riutta**, a resident of Gaylord, Michigan, is a chef and Zamboni driver. In 2012 his essay, "The Myths of Manhood," was featured on PRI's *Bob Edwards Show*.

A former president of the Haiku Society of America, **Ce Rosenow**'s books include *The Backs of Angels, Even If, North Lake, Pacific, Spectral Forms*, and *A Year Longer*. She is one of the eight authors of *Beyond Within: A Collection of Rengay* and co-editor, with Bob Arnold, of *The Next One Thousand Years: Selected Poems of Cid Corman*.

A licensed acupuncturist and digital artist who lives in Winston-Salem, North Carolina, **Alexis Rotella**'s latest books include *Scratches on the Moon* (haibun), and *Dancing the Tarantella* (tanka/cherita). She edited and curated *Unsealing Our Secrets* anthology (MeToo stories in short-form poetry), which was awarded a Touchstone Book Award for 2018.

Native New Yorker **Robert Rotella** spent over 50 years as an intellectual property attorney. Haiku helps him fine tune his legal writings.

Natalia L Rudychev, a Fulbright scholar, is also an award-winning photographer, and Touchstone Distinguished Books Award shortlisted poet. Natalia's work appeared in many journals including *Ribbons, Gusts, Red Lights, Blythe Spirit, Tanka International*, and *Modern English Tanka*.

Miriam Sagan is the author of thirty books of poetry, fiction, and memoir. She created the haiku pathway at Santa Fe Community College — 40 haiku poets on stoneware in the central courtyard.

Wisconsin-born **Dan Schwerin** is a grandfather whose poems come out of life lived on farms, in rural towns, suburbs, and the city. Dan is a shepherd of United Methodist congregations and facilitates the monthly meeting of Haiku Waukesha.

Adelaide B Shaw lives in Somers, NY where she has been writing haiku, tanka and other short form Japanese poetry for nearly 50 years. Her work has appeared in numerous journals in the US and abroad. *www.adelaide-whitepetals.blogspot.com.*

Caroline Skanne was born in Sweden and now lives by the river Medway in Kent, UK. She is the founder of the short-poetry journal *hedgerow* and the current editor of *Blithe Spirit. carolineskanne.com* & on Instagram *carolineskannehaikuetc.*

A former vice president of the Tanka Society of America and resident of Massachusetts, where he lives with his wife and cat, **Ken Slaughter**'s tanka have been published in many online and print journals.

In 2015, he won first prize in the Tanka Society of America annual contest.

A resident of Northern California and retired registered nurse, **Cindy Smith** pursues passions, which include reading, writing and photography. She's an avid seeker of beautiful light, prose from her soul, and a keeper of magical moments only grandchildren can give.

Short-form poet and lover of old-time blues, **Paul Smith** lives with his wife and family in Worcester, UK. He delights in building cigar box guitars, using mostly recycled parts.

Christina Sng is an award-winning poet, writer, and artist. Her books include the Bram Stoker Award winning *A Collection of Nightmares* and Elgin runner-up *Astropoetry*.

Sheila Sondik, poet and printmaker, lives and works in Bellingham, Washington, surrounded by the Pacific Northwest's natural beauty. A long-time lover of haiku, she has been writing haiku and tanka since 2010.

Carmen Sterba first went to Japan in 1965 and wound up living, studying and teaching there for 32 years. During that time she got interested in Japanese poetry, including tanka, in the early 2000s and found that classic tanka was a way to send notes to lovers.

John Stevenson (born 1948, Ithaca, NY) is a former president of the Haiku Society of America. He edited *Frogpond* from 2005-2007 and has been the managing editor of *The Heron's Nest* since 2008.

Maria Steyn lives in Johannesburg, South Africa. Her tanka have been published in *Ribbons, Eucalypt, Gusts, Kokako, Magnapoets* and other international publications. Her tanka sequence with Beverley George is published in *wind through the wheatfields* (2012).

A resident of the United Kingdom who earned a PhD in theology, **Iliyana Stoyanova**'s haiku and other poems have been published in numerous journals and anthologies, and won several international awards. She enjoys photography, watercolor painting, traveling, and reading.

Debbie Strange is an internationally published short-form poet and haiga artist. She recently won the Sable Books Women's Haiku Contest for her forthcoming manuscript, *The Language of Loss: Haiku and Tanka Conversations.*

Celia Stuart-Powles began writing haiku about 1994 and attended the Global Haiku Conference in 2000 where she became a founding member of the Tanka Society of America, and much later served as its secretary.

From England, **Alan Summers** is President of the United Haiku and Tanka Society; a double *Japan Times* award-winning writer; and a Pushcart Prize and Best Small Fictions nominated poet. He is co-founder of Call of the Page: *www.callofthepage.org.*

Carmel Summers is a Canberra poet, with work published in anthologies and journals in Australia and overseas. Her collaborative book, *The last day before snow*, was awarded the ACT Publishers Poetry Award in 2017.

A resident of eastern Pennsylvania, **Lesley Anne Swanson** has won many awards for her tanka, some of which include: First Place, Tanka Society of America (2014); First Place (Certificate of Merit) Japan Poets' Society (2012, 2016), and International Tanka Festival Competitions.

David Terelinck likes gin and tonic and believes dolphins should be running the planet.

Michael Thorley lives his life mainly in Canberra, Australia. He writes all forms of poetry and in later years has become a Japanophile.

Julie Thorndyke lives and works in Sydney. Editor of *Eucalypt*, a tanka journal, since 2017, she also writes fiction, picture books and other poetry forms. Visit her at *https://jthorndyke.wordpress.com*.

A retired university professor and editor/publisher of *Gusts*, the journal of Tanka Canada, **Kozue Uzawa** has lived in Canada since 1971. She has published two tanka translation books: *Ferris Wheel*, a collection of modern tanka, and *Kaleidoscope — Tanka of Shuji Terayama. Ferris Wheel*

Margaret Van Every lives in the mountains of central Mexico where she's an active member of The Not Yet Dead Poets' Society. She writes poetry, short fiction, and essays and has three books of poetry on Amazon.

Editor of *Ribbons*, **Christine "Chrissi" L. Villa** is an award-winning tanka and haiku poet. She is the founding editor of *Frameless Sky*, the first haiku and tanka journal available on DVD, and of Velvet Dusk Publishing. *www.christinevilla.com*.

Tamara K Walker is a writer and poet who works in several English-language adaptations of Asian forms, primarily including tanka, sijo and ghazal. Her debut chapbook, *Fabric Heart: A Collection of Contemporary Introspective Sijo*, was published by Finishing Line Press (2019). *tamarakwalker.weebly.com*.

Karma Tenzing Wangchuk is the author of several books of haiku and three short collections of tanka: *Clouds Gather and Part* (Tel-Let, 2004), *Songs from a Cricket Cage* (Tribe Press, 2006), and *Open Door: Love Poems* (Privately printed, 2013). He has been active in social justice, environmental, war resistance, and other causes since the late 1950s.

Linda Jeannette Ward has published two collections of tanka: *A Frayed Red Thread* (Clinging Vine Press, 2000) and *Scent of Jasmine and Brine* (Inkling Press, 2007). She has won first prize for her tanka in several international competitions.

Michael Dylan Welch founded the Tanka Society of America (*www.tankasocietyofamerica.org*) in 2000 and is currently its president. He has served two terms as poet laureate of Redmond, Washington. *www.graceguts.com*.

Don Wentworth writes poetry that reflects his interest in the revelatory nature of brief, numinous moments in everyday life. He is the author of three full-length collections from Six Gallery Press. Forthcoming books include collections of ghazals from Low Ghost Press and haiku from Lascaux Editions.

Neal Whitman lives on California's Monterey Peninsula where he and his wife have learned that, if you're lucky enough to live by the ocean, you are lucky enough. Neal finds inspiration for his poetry in ancient poetry put into written text such as the *Man'yōshū* 1300 years ago and the *Iliad* 2700 years ago.

Published in numerous places, **Steve Wilkinson** has been writing short form poetry since before the internet arrived. He is editor of the tanshi journal *The Bamboo Hut*.

A colorful figure who considers poetry as a power for repair, **Kath Abela Wilson** sailed past the Statue of Liberty in New York Bay and its liberating poem a thousand times on the ferry from her childhood home to Manhattan. Her mother, who inspired many poems, saw America as a haven for peace.

Working on a novel, **Beatrice Yell** was born in Sydney and lives on its northern beaches. Introduced to the delights of tanka some years ago, she still finds it both a challenge and a joy. Her work appears in several international publications.

Aya Yuhki is president of the International Tanka Society and publisher of International Tanka. Translations include *Selected Tanka and Poems of Aya Yuhki* in Japanese and English.

J Zimmerman was the TSA book reviewer for *Ribbons* (2017 – 2019). Featured in *A New Resonance 8* (Red Moon Press, 2013), she was first Poet in Residence for the Cabrillo Festival of Contemporary Music (2014).

Made in the USA
Columbia, SC
29 October 2022

70186934R00126